What To Do With A Squirt Of Glue

and Paper, Paint and Scissors, Too!

by
Lori A. Howard

Incentive Publications, Inc.
Nashville, Tennessee

Illustrations and cover by Susan Eaddy
Edited by Jennifer Goodman

Library of Congress Catalog Card Number 86-82518
ISBN 0-86530-086-0

TABLE OF CONTENTS

INTRODUCTION

WHAT TO DO WITH A SQUIRT OF GLUE is for teachers, parents, caregivers or anyone else who is interested in providing enriching and creative art experiences for children. Art is more than a segregated discipline. It is an integral part of the whole educational process and is vital to the child's total well-being. Art provides a vehicle for discovery, self-expression and the opportunity for self-paced growth. The creative thinking and feeling fostered through artistic endeavors is manifested not only in the child's artwork but in his social, emotional, physical and mental development as well.

This book has been conveniently divided into chapters by predominant art media. Each chapter offers many projects and techniques as well as alternative ways of exploring the various materials. Suitable for children of any age, the activities included are simple enough for a "non-artist" to conduct. They may be carried out individually or with small groups of children. Some can be done spontaneously while others require minimal advance planning. Although variety tends to stimulate interest, don't be reluctant to return to favored activities. Remember, children build on repetition as well as experience. As you try some of these activities you'll probably invent new ways of expanding on the original ideas. Please do! The emphasis here is on the experiential approach to learning where the process is of more importance than the final product.

Most importantly, remember that it is through you, the adult in charge, that children will learn and develop attitudes about art and creativity which will stay with them for the rest of their lives. You can exert a positive influence by providing an atmosphere to enhance creative thinking; by allowing children to explore freely the use and possibilities of various art media; by providing a variety of materials and activities to enable children to select the media best suited to their individual needs; and by giving praise and encouragement to nurture the natural creative drive.

SUPPLIES OF GREAT IMPORTANCE

PAINT
- liquid tempera
- powdered tempera
- watercolors

GLUE
Buy school glue in large quantities and pour into squeeze bottles or covered margarine tubs. (Keep covered when not in use.)

TAPE
- masking
- cellophane
- colored

BRUSHES
- wide, flat easel brushes
- small watercolor brushes
- glue brushes

SCISSORS
Safe, non-breakable safety scissors are the best. They can be used by either left or right-handed children. Children can easily put two fingers in the openings.

FOODS
- flour
- salt
- cornstarch
- oatmeal
- rice
- vegetable oil
- food colors
- liquid starch

NEEDLES
Extra large plastic or metal embroidery needles with blunt ends.

MEDICINE DROPPERS
Make sure they are cleaned thoroughly before using.

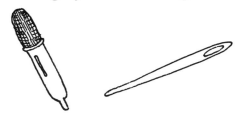

WRITING UTENSILS
- crayons
- markers (water base)
- felt-tip marking pens
- pencils and colored pencils
- chalk

PASTE
Purchase school paste or make your own.

PAPER
- newsprint 18" x 24"
- construction paper 12" x 18"
- Manila drawing paper
- butcher paper
- wrapping paper
- wallpaper
- tissue paper
- wax paper
- foil
- crepe paper

SPECIAL THINGS TO SAVE

acorns
berry baskets
bottle caps
buttons/beads/broken jewelry
cardboard
cardboard tubes
chestnuts
clothespins
coffee cans
corks
cottage cheese containers
cotton balls
cotton swabs
divided snack tins
empty boxes of all sizes
feathers
felt
frozen juice cans
gears
grocery bags
macaroni
magazines
margarine tubs
material scraps
newspapers
old combs

old cupcake tins
old puzzle pieces
old shirts for smocks
old toothbrushes
old toy pieces
paper clips
pie tins
pine cones
plastic lids
popsicle sticks
seeds
shells
shoe boxes
socks
spice jars and cans
spools
squeeze bottles
string
Styrofoam egg cartons
Styrofoam meat trays
Styrofoam packing pieces
wallpaper sample books
wrapping paper scraps
wood scraps
yarns
yogurt containers

CHECK commercial firms for some of these free or inexpensive items.

APPLIANCE STORE - large cardboard boxes
COMPUTER FIRM - punchouts, paper
CONTRACTOR - large blueprint paper
DRY CLEANERS - shirt cardboards
ICE CREAM PARLOR - large round cartons
NEWSPAPER COMPANY - paper roll ends
PRINTING FIRM - scrap paper
TELEPHONE COMPANY - colored wire, wooden spools
TEXTILE COMPANY - fabric scraps, trims, buttons, spools
WOOD OR LUMBER MILL - sawdust, wood scraps, sandpaper belts

CAUTION

Make sure that all materials you choose are clean and safe for children to use. Watch out for sharp or pointed edges.

SETTING UP AN ART AREA

An ideal art area should be located in an uncongested area, preferably one with a washable table and floor, a sink and ample storage space. If setting up an art area in the home or where these conditions can't be met, please take the following necessary precautions:

- Choose a place that will allow adequate freedom for experimentation and where the children can work with no fear of damaging things.

- Protect the table and floor from spills and drips. This can be done by spreading out newspapers, an old plastic tablecloth or an old shower curtain.

- Choose appropriate furniture such as a small, low table and a stool or chair. Move all other furniture out of the way if possible.

- Provide old clothes or smocks to protect clothing. An old shirt worn backwards is perfect. Make sure to roll up sleeves.

- If a sink isn't nearby, provide a washtub and paper towels for quick cleanup of hands, spills and supplies.

- Make sure that children have a specific place to keep art supplies. Store in boxes, plastic tubs, and cans in a way that is both convenient and readily accessible. It is helpful to categorize and label materials accordingly. Make sure to keep toxic items out of reach and bring them out only when you can supervise their use.

- Have a space set aside for drying finished artwork. This doesn't have to be shelf space. A plastic or wooden clothes dryer or a clothesline will suffice. Remember to protect the floor under your drying area.

- A special box decorated by children themselves or a portfolio purchased at an art supply store can be used to store finished artwork. These projects have a tendency to accumulate rather quickly so sort them often, saving those that are most special. (Remember, it is the process and not the product that is of the utmost importance.)

IMPLEMENTATION

- Once an art area is established, make sure to set limits for the use of materials. Be fair and firm. For example, if children are allowed to paint in certain designated areas, make sure they understand when and under what circumstances it is acceptable to do so.

- Secure and prepare all materials in advance. Exercise a concern for safety in the choice of materials. Experiment with them yourself using different sizes, shapes, colors and textures. This should help you assess more realistically the limitations of certain materials with different age groups and for different projects.

- The amount of teacher assistance will depend on the abilities of the children. Allow them to do as much as they can unassisted and intervene only when necessary.

- The finished product need not be perfect so try to focus attention on the process rather than the completed work. The seemingly abstract scribbles and forms are often indecipherable to the adult but tend to be of great significance to the child.

- Children want their work to be accepted so don't forget to supply lots of praise and encouragement. Your praise should serve to build up the child's confidence so that he is motivated to experiment further.

- Involve children as much as possible in preparation and cleanup tasks. This not only saves valuable time, it also makes the total experience more child oriented and therefore more meaningful.

WAYS WITH PAINT

PAINTING

SUPPLIES

- any water base paint such as tempera or poster paint
- empty containers for small amount of paint (juice cans work well)
- brushes, all sizes, preferably ½" - 1" wide
- paper
- container of water for cleaning brushes

PREPARATION

- Pour paints into individual containers choosing only two or three different colors (primary colors - red, yellow and blue will make almost any other color). If using powdered tempera, mix with water until it is thick and creamy.
- Put a brush in each color if possible.
- Place the containers in a muffin tin or cardboard soda carton to prevent tipping.

LET'S BEGIN

1. Place a sheet of paper on table (or an easel) with two or three colors of paint. With very young children one color at a time might be enough.
2. Dip the brush into the paint and apply it to the paper. Explore and mix the colors until picture is finished. This might be only after a few brush strokes or it might be after the entire paper is covered.
3. Notice what happens when colors are mixed.
4. When finished, wash the brush with soap and water and put the painting away to dry.

OTHER IDEAS

- Try changing the texture of the paint. To thin, add a lot of water. To thicken, add soap flakes, sand, sawdust or coffee grounds.

WHAT CAN YOU PAINT WITH?

Sometimes it's fun to try painting with
other things besides brushes.
Why not try:

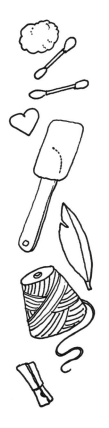

- **Cotton swabs**
  (good for making dots)
- **Toothpicks**
  (for tiny lines)
- **Flowers**
  (Queen Anne's Lace
  makes beautiful lacy
  snowflake-like designs)
- **Spatulas**
- **String**
  (for swirls and drips)
- **Cotton balls**
  (hold onto them with
  clothespins)

- **Forks**
  (for multiple lines)
- **Spoons**
- **Butter knife**
  (for spreading)
- **Sticks**
  (choose ones with little
  branches for
  interesting lines)
- **Popsicle sticks** or
  tongue depressors
- **Sponges**
- **Cardboard pieces**
- **Feathers**

WHAT CAN YOU PAINT ON?

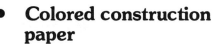

- **Colored construction
  paper**
- **Gauze or cheesecloth**
  (A very absorbent
  surface that creates a
  soft effect when painted
  on.)
- **Brown paper bags**
- **Paper towels**
  (Paint on directly or
  fold and dip into paint.)
- **White butcher paper**
- **Newspapers**
  (These make interesting
  patterns when painted
  on.)
- **Manila drawing paper**
- **Sandpaper**

- **T-Shirts**
  (Use fabric or acrylic
  paints - both are water
  base. Make sure to slip
  a cardboard or paper
  piece inside the shirt
  before you start.)
- **Newsprint**
- **Windows**
  (Add a little liquid
  detergent to tempera
  paint and paint directly
  on the windowpane.)
- **Muslin**
  (Or solid color cotton
  material.)
- **Bodies**
  (Use finger paints with
  a little liquid detergent.)

HOMEMADE FINGER PAINT

Recipe #1
Mix 1 cup of liquid starch with 1 cup of powdered tempera paint or ½ cup of liquid tempera.

Recipe #2
Mix ½ cup of soap flakes with ½ cup of liquid tempera paint. Add ½ cup of liquid starch. This finger paint will be thicker than recipe #1.

Recipe #3
Mix 1 cup flour and 3 cups water and stir over medium heat until it boils. It will turn transparent. Turn off heat and let mixture cool. Add coloring (either liquid or powdered tempera). Store in covered container in the refrigerator if it is to be kept longer than a couple of days.

CAUTION
Some children will not want to use finger paints for fear of getting dirty. Remember that they were probably told to keep clean and they don't want to get "messed up." Don't force the child to indulge but encourage him to use only one finger or a comb until he feels more comfortable with this activity.

FINGER PAINTING

SUPPLIES

- finger paint (Buy this at any art supply store or make your own. See recipes pg. 16.)
- finger paint paper or shiny shelf paper
- container of water
- large spoon

PREPARATION

- Make finger paint if not using store-bought.

LET'S BEGIN

1. Dampen paper with sprinkles of water. (Younger students may want to pretend it is rain.)
2. Place a spoonful of paint on the paper and spread it around with fingers, opened hands, fingernails and fists.
3. Play with the paint, making pictures and designs. Add a second color and mix. Be careful not to overwork paper or it will rip!
4. When finished, clean up and put the paintings away to dry.

OTHER IDEAS

- Use other objects such as combs or cardboard pieces.
- Make a print from the finished painting by placing another sheet of paper on top of it. Press and remove. This will make a mirror image.
- If a linoleum covered table is available, finger paint right on the table top. Take a print of the painting when finished.
- Shake on a little glitter while painting is still wet.

Look! It's raining on my paper!

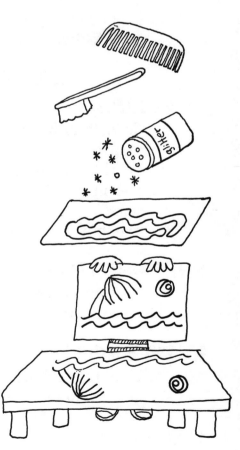

EDIBLE FINGER PAINT

PUDDING

SUPPLIES
- instant pudding - any flavor, but chocolate seems to be the all-time favorite
- milk
- bowl for mixing
- spoon
- paper

PREPARATION
- Make pudding according to package directions. If using vanilla, add food color.

LET'S BEGIN
Proceed the same way as in regular finger painting but this time allow students to lick their fingers.

JELLO

SUPPLIES
- Jello (any flavor)
- water
- bowl for mixing
- spoon
- paper
- brushes

PREPARATION
- Mix small amounts of the Jello with warm water until it turns slushy.

LET'S BEGIN
Use this as finger paint or brush it on like shiny watercolors.

CAUTION
Be aware of food allergies. Many children are allergic to chocolate or artificial flavorings.

BAG PAINTING

SUPPLIES
- finger paint
- Ziploc storage bags
- masking tape
- paper

PREPARATION
- Pour about ¼ cup of finger paint into a Ziploc storage bag.
- Close and seal the bag, making sure all the air is out. Tape top to prevent opening.

LET'S BEGIN
1. Lay the bag down on top of a sheet of paper. (If using dark colored paint, use a light sheet of paper; if using light colored paint, use dark paper.)
2. Using fingers, paint on top of the bag as in regular finger painting.
3. Lift up the bag and let paint collect back in the bottom to make the painting disappear.
4. Repeat the procedure over and over to make as many paintings as desired.

OTHER IDEAS
- Pour two colors of paint into the Ziploc bag. Proceed as above. Watch the paints mix into a new color.

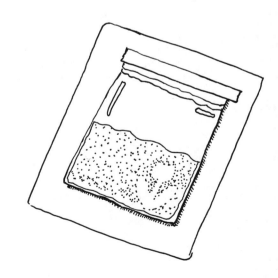

ROLL-ON PAINTING

SUPPLIES
- empty roll-on deodorant bottles with removable tops
- tempera paint thinned with water
- paper

PREPARATION
- Pry tops off of clean, roll-on bottles.
- Fill bottles with thinned paint and replace tops.

LET'S BEGIN
1. Tip up bottle and press onto a sheet of paper. Roll paint in designs, swirls, letters or shapes.
2. Use other colors if available.
3. When finished, allow paint to dry.
4. Screw covers on bottles to keep paint from drying out.

CAUTION
- If using glass bottles make sure children don't hit them hard on the table or they might break.

WATERCOLOR PAINTING

SUPPLIES
- watercolor paints (any kind)
- brushes
- paper
- container for water

PREPARATION
- If using tube watercolors, squeeze out paints into small dishes or muffin tins and add a little water.

LET'S BEGIN
1. Dip the brush in water and in the paint, turning the paint into little puddles.
2. Brush the paint from the puddles onto a piece of paper in thin coats.
3. Remember, these are watercolors, not tempera paints, and have a transparent look when applied to paper. (I call them see-through paints.)
4. When finished painting, wash out brush and put paintings away to dry.

OTHER IDEAS
- Try wetting paper first with a sponge. Paint over dampened paper. The colors will spread over the paper into interesting washes.
- While paint is still wet, try sprinkling salt on top. The salt will absorb the watercolors and leave areas of sparkled color.
- Try drawing a picture with crayons. Then paint over the entire paper with watercolors. The wax in the crayons will cause what is called a "resist painting."
- Draw a picture with markers or felt-tip pens and then paint over the drawing. The marker lines will blur, producing an interesting effect.

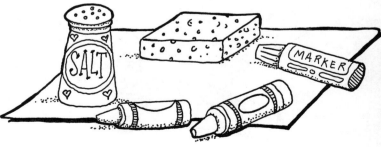

BLOTTO PAINTING

SUPPLIES
- tempera paint
- brushes
- paper
- container of water for cleaning brushes

PREPARATION
- Pour paints into individual containers.
- Provide brushes and water for cleaning them.

LET'S BEGIN
1. Fold a piece of paper in half.
2. Open up paper and paint a picture or design on one side only.
3. Fold paper again and press gently.
4. Open up paper to see design.
5. Put paintings away to dry when finished.

OTHER IDEAS
- Cut paper into small shapes and make blotto paintings. When finished arrange and glue them onto another sheet of paper.

COLORED SAND PAINTING

SUPPLIES
- sand (without pebbles, sticks or leaves)
- powdered tempera paint
- glue
- glue brushes
- spoons
- paper (dark colors usually work best)
- containers (such as empty cottage cheese containers) for mixing sand paint

PREPARATION
- Put sand in container and add a little powdered tempera. Stir until sand and paint are well mixed, adding more paint if necessary.
- Pour glue into glue cup.

LET'S BEGIN
1. Brush design on paper with glue.
2. Take spoon and sprinkle colored sand over glued area.
3. Pour excess sand off of paper and back into container.
4. Brush on more glue and add a different color of sand.
5. When picture is finished put it away to dry.

OTHER IDEAS
- Instead of brushing on glue, put glue into a squirt bottle and squeeze on a design - the thin lines make an interesting picture.
- Put the leftover colored sand in a clear plastic container such as a plastic drinking cup. Alternate layers of different colors. These layered sand designs don't usually last too long but are fun never-the-less.

23

PASTE PAINTING

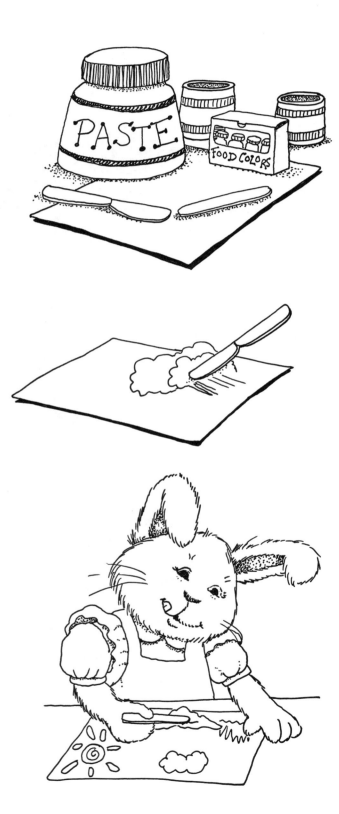

SUPPLIES
- paste
- tempera paint or food colors
- containers for mixing paste paint
- spoons
- tongue depressors or plastic butter knives
- paper

PREPARATION
- Spoon paste into individual containers.
- Add coloring and stir until mixed (you may need to thin with a little water).

LET'S BEGIN
1. Spoon a small amount of colored paste on the paper.
2. Use the tongue depressor or knife to spread the paste into a picture or design and add texture.
3. Add another color to overlap with the first color.
4. When finished, let dry.

OTHER IDEAS
- Try making imprints in the paste paint with different gadgets such as pennies, buttons, pieces of burlap, toothpicks, cookie cutters, etc.

COLORED GLUE PAINTING

SUPPLIES
- glue
- food colors or tempera paint
- containers for mixing glue paint
- brushes
- water
- paper

PREPARATION
- Pour glue into container.
- Add a few drops of color and mix.
- Add a little water to thin out and mix again.
- Repeat for every color used.

LET'S BEGIN
1. Lay out paper.
2. Brush on glue paint as if using regular tempera paint.
3. Mix colors together.
4. When finished, let dry.

OTHER IDEAS
- Glue paint makes interesting paintings on foil and Mylar, too!
- Try using it on wax paper. Hang in window when dry for a see-through painting.

DROPPER PAINTING

SUPPLIES
- eye droppers (If using old medicine droppers make sure they are thoroughly cleaned.)
- tempera paint
- containers for paint
- paper
- water

PREPARATION
- Pour paints into individual containers and thin with water until they are quite thin.

LET'S BEGIN
1. Fill dropper with thinned paint.
2. Squeeze drops of paint onto paper to make drips and splashes.
3. Try overlapping colors.
4. When finished, let paintings dry and wash out droppers thoroughly.

CAUTION
- Try not to touch the tip of the dropper on the paper as it may get clogged.

SMUDGE PAINTING

SUPPLIES
- plastic flat covers or lids (transparent is best)
- tempera paint
- brushes
- containers for paint and water
- paper

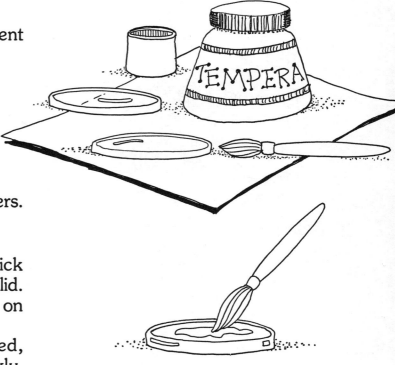

PREPARATION
- Pour paints into individual containers.

LET'S BEGIN
1. Turn lid flat side down. Apply a thick coat of paint on a small area of the lid.
2. Choose another color and brush on unpainted area.
3. Add another color if desired, remembering to apply paint thickly.
4. Turn painted cover upside down on the paper.
5. Press down on cover, rub gently, and lift quickly. The paint should make a very interesting textural design.
6. Repeat procedure as many times as necessary to cover the entire paper.
7. When finished, allow paintings to dry.

OTHER IDEAS
- Instead of lifting the painting cover off the paper, perform quick sliding or twisting movements to produce spiral designs.

SPATTER PAINTING

SUPPLIES

- thinned tempera paint
- old toothbrush
- window screening
- paper
- containers for paint
- masking tape

PREPARATION

- Prepare screen by cutting into pieces about 6" x 6".
- Apply masking tape around the edges of the screen so there are no sharp edges.
- Pour paints into individual containers.

LET'S BEGIN

1. Hold the spatter paint screen over a sheet of paper.
2. Dip the toothbrush into the paint and rub it across the top of the screen to produce spatters on the paper below.
3. Dip the toothbrush into another color and spatter on top of first color.
4. When finished, allow paintings to dry. Wash screen and toothbrushes.

OTHER IDEAS

- Cut patterns or stencils from paper or cardboard. Place the stencil on a piece of paper. When finished, remove stencils.
- Rub a stick across the toothbrush while holding it face down over some paper.
- Embroidery hoop frames with plastic screen wire also work well as spatter paint frames.

STRING PAINTING

SUPPLIES
- several pieces of string about 12" long
- tempera paint
- paper
- container for paint (a low flat dish such as a Styrofoam tray works best)
- clothespins (optional)

PREPARATION
- Cut string into 12" pieces.
- Pour paints into trays.

LET'S BEGIN
1. Hold on to one end of a piece of string and dip it in the paint. (Use a clothespin for a handle.)
2. Make designs by dragging the painted string across the paper.
3. For different effects try snapping it, swinging it or making a specific shape by laying it down on the paper and pulling it up.
4. Use one color of paint or several strings with different colors.
5. Put paper away to dry when finished.

OTHER IDEAS
- Fold paper in half. Dip string in paint and lay down on one half of the paper. (Make sure that the end of the string hangs out of the folded paper.) Press down gently on top of the paper with one hand as you carefully pull the string out. Unfold the paper to see the design you created.

BLOW PAINTING

SUPPLIES
- tempera paint
- plastic drinking straws
- paper
- spoons
- containers for paints

PREPARATION
- Thin paints with water and pour into containers.
- Cut straws in half to make blowing easier.

LET'S BEGIN
1. Spoon a blob of paint on paper.
2. Hold end of straw close to the paint but don't touch it!
3. Blow into straw to spread paint in all directions.
4. Blow on another color for mixed color effects.
5. Use as many colors as desired.
6. Put away to dry when finished.

OTHER IDEAS
- Blow paintings look like fireworks when done on black paper. Using black paint on orange paper produces "Halloween spiders."

CAUTION
- Make sure children are blowing and not sucking on the straws. This activity tends to make one light-headed if done for a long time so make sure to take frequent breaks.

MARBLE PAINTING

SUPPLIES
- tempera paint
- marbles (the largest size you can find)
- shoe box, pie tin or tray with sides
- spoons
- containers for paint
- paper

PREPARATION
- Pour paints into containers.
- Cut paper to fit inside box or tin.

LET'S BEGIN
1. Put sheet of paper in box.
2. Drop marble into paint container.
3. Spoon marble out of paint and drop in box.
4. Tilt box from side to side to roll the marble across the paper.
5. Dip marble in other colors and repeat process until painting is finished.
6. Take paper out of box and let dry.

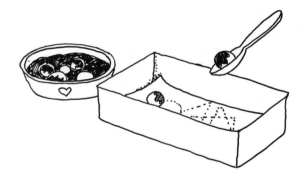

OTHER IDEAS
- Cut paper into different shapes before putting them in the box. Marble paint on them as above.
- A similar painting can be made without marbles. Drop very wet paint on paper. Pick up paper and tilt from side to side or back and forth, forming designs as the paint runs.

SWIRL PAINTING

SUPPLIES
- vegetable oil
- powdered tempera paint
- paper
- shallow pan (such as a pie tin)
- water
- spoons
- containers for paint
- clothespins (optional)

PREPARATION
- In small container, mix powdered tempera paint with some vegetable oil until creamy. Prepare at least two colors (the more the better) in separate containers.
- Cut paper to fit inside of pan.
- Fill pan with water about ½" - 1" deep.

LET'S BEGIN
1. Spoon a few drops of each color vegetable oil paint on top of the water in the pan.
2. Take another spoon or stick and swirl.
3. Lay a piece of paper on top of the water and let sit for a minute.
4. Lift off the paper to get a swirled painting.
5. When finished, allow paintings to dry. Wash spoons and trays.

OTHER IDEAS
- Clip a clothespin on the edge of the paper to use as a handle when lifting paper from water.
- Try turning the paper while it is lying on the water before lifting out.

SCRIBBLES AND SQUIGGLES

CRAYONS

Crayons are probably the most familiar of all the art materials. They work well on most papers and are clean, colorful and inexpensive. They come in various kinds and sizes. The jumbo size is usually the best for younger children. Crayons are most effective with their jackets off!

VARIATIONS ON A CRAYON
*This is a teacher or parent process

1. Save old broken pieces of crayons.
2. Put like-colored crayon pieces in a clean tin can.
3. Place tin can in pan of water and bring to a boil.

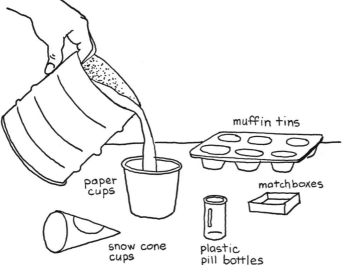

paper cups

muffin tins

matchboxes

snow cone cups

plastic pill bottles

4. The wax should begin to boil. Watch it carefully as wax is highly flammable.
5. When wax cools slightly, pour into one of the containers pictured.
6. When hardened, dip the container quickly into hot water to remove wax crayon.

OTHER IDEAS
• To make a rainbow crayon, pour different colors of melted crayons into a mold, swirl and let harden. Or, make layers of melted crayon and let each layer harden before pouring on next color.

34

CRAYON TEXTURE RUBBING

SUPPLIES
- crayons with jackets removed
- lightweight paper (newsprint)
- interesting surfaces

LET'S BEGIN
1. Place a sheet of paper over a surface which has an interesting texture.
2. Lay the crayon on its side and rub over the paper.
3. The surface texture will appear on the paper.

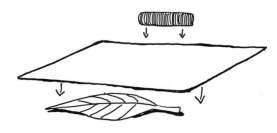

OTHER IDEAS
- Do rubbings using various flat items with interesting textures such as leaves, coins, open weave material, sandpaper, bark, combs, etc.
- Go on a texture hike around the room, playground or neighborhood. Rub as many different textures as possible and staple the pages into a book.
- Do rubbings of cutout cardboard shapes or stencils. Take rubbings of soles of shoes, labels, zippers, buttons, etc.
- Make a secret rubbing by putting a flat "mystery object" in an envelope. Give this to someone to rub to reveal what is inside.

CRAYON RESIST

SUPPLIES
- wax crayons
- watercolor paints
- paper
- brush
- container for water

LET'S BEGIN
1. Draw a picture or design on paper. Make sure to press down hard and to leave some of the paper blank.
2. Cover the entire paper with one or several colors of watercolor paint. The paint will be resisted by the crayon and will only color the blank areas of the picture.

OTHER IDEAS
- Do a magic picture by drawing on white paper with a white crayon. The picture will be almost invisible. Next, paint over the entire sheet of paper with watercolor paints and the crayoned picture will appear. This is fun for sending secret messages to friends or family.
- An underwater effect can be created by painting blue watercolor paints over sea life crayon drawings.
- These projects can be done by using a bar of soap instead of crayons.

SEE-THROUGH PICTURES

SUPPLIES
- crayons
- white paper
- vegetable oil or baby oil
- cotton balls

LET'S BEGIN
1. Draw shapes and designs on a sheet of paper by pressing down hard with crayons.
2. Fill in as much space as possible with solid colors.
3. When the drawing has been completed, use a cotton ball and rub oil over the back of the paper.
4. The crayon picture from the front will now appear on the back of the paper (backwards!).

CRAYON ETCHING

SUPPLIES
- wax crayons
- heavy paper that will withstand the etching process
- sharp-pointed object such as a stick or hairpin
- India ink (black)
- talcum powder

LET'S BEGIN
1. Using crayons, cover an entire sheet of paper with several bright colors. (Avoid using black!)
2. Cover the colored surface with a black crayon until none of the colors show through and the paper is completely black.

    or

    Dust the crayon-colored surface with talcum powder and paint over with India ink. Allow the ink to dry before going on to the next step.
3. Using a sharp pointed object, scratch a design or picture into the black crayon or ink. The colorful pattern underneath will show through.

DRAWING WITH CHALK

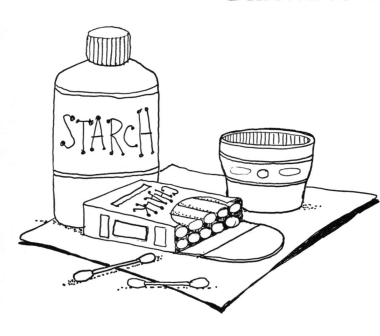

SUPPLIES
- package of colored chalk
- paper
- liquid starch or sugar water (for a more brilliant line)
- cotton swab
- container for starch

PREPARATION
- Pour a small amount of liquid starch into a container.

LET'S BEGIN
1. Dip a piece of chalk into the liquid starch and make a drawing.
2. Using a cotton swab or a finger, rub the chalk lines to make a smeared effect.
3. Place two colors side by side and rub them together.

WET PAPER CHALK DRAWING

SUPPLIES
- package of colored chalk
- paper
- container of water
- sponge (optional)

LET'S BEGIN
1. Dampen paper with water.
2. While paper is still wet, color a design or picture. The wet paper makes the colors seem more brilliant and less likely to brush off.

CAUTION
- Be careful when drawing on wet paper as it tears easily.

CHALK AND TEMPERA

SUPPLIES
- package of colored chalk
- white tempera paint
- paper
- brush

PREPARATION
- Pour white paint into container.

LET'S BEGIN
1. Make a colored chalk drawing on a piece of paper. Be sure to press down hard with the chalk.
2. Take another piece of paper of the same size and brush white tempera over its entire surface.
3. While paint is still wet, place the chalk drawing face down on the painted paper.
4. Lift off the top piece and see the results.

CHALK ON STYRO

SUPPLIES
- Styrofoam meat packaging tray
- package of colored chalk
- starch
- small container for starch
- paper

PREPARATION
- Pour liquid starch into container.
- Cut edges off the meat tray to make it flat.

LET'S BEGIN
1. Brush liquid starch over the entire surface of the meat tray.
2. Using chalk, draw a picture on top of the starched tray.
3. Brush top of chalk picture with more liquid starch.
4. Place chalk picture on a piece of paper and rub gently.
5. Lift up tray to see picture.
6. Repeat process until paper is covered.

WET MARKERS

SUPPLIES
- water base markers
- finger paint paper or smooth shelf paper (allows markers to easily glide over the smooth surface)
- container of water

LET'S BEGIN
1. Dip the marker into the water.
2. Draw on the paper. Make sure to overlap colors.
3. When finished, put paper away to dry.

OTHER IDEAS
- Make a drawing with water base markers. Take a brush and brush over the drawing with water. This will produce an effect similar to a watercolor painting.

CAUTION
- Make sure to keep the covers on the markers so they won't dry out. Temporarily revive markers with removable ends by taking off the end cap and placing a few drops of vinegar into the marker shaft. Recap and shake and marker should work again.

Take off this end

STICKY SITUATIONS

COLLAGE

Collage is a French word meaning "to paste" or "to stick." A collage is a picture of different things stuck together. It can be planned to suggest a subject or be abstract. Anything that can be glued to paper or cardboard can be used. For example:

all kinds of paper scraps
magazine pictures
fabric scraps
strings and yarns
beans, seeds, nuts
macaroni shapes
sawdust
broken jewelry beads
pebbles
straws
wallpaper samples
computer punchouts
eggshells
aluminum foil
cellophane
broken toys and games
buttons
bottle caps
seashells
shoelaces

SUPPLIES
- paper or cardboard for background
- selected collage items
- glue
- scissors

LET'S BEGIN
1. Choose items from the collage treasures collected.
2. Arrange and glue selected objects onto the paper.
3. Let dry.

OTHER IDEAS
- For an interesting change, add food color or tempera paint to change the color of the glue.
- Coffee cans or shoe boxes are good for storing collage materials.

SOME COLLAGE THEMES

NATURE COLLAGE
Collect things found out-of-doors (leaves, acorns, twigs, nuts, etc.) and glue together for a nature collage. Instead of using paper for a background try using a large piece of bark or wood.

BREAKFAST COLLAGE
Use different kinds of cereals to make this collage. Cut apart a cereal box and use as the background.

A SHAPE COLLAGE
Focus on only one shape such as a triangle. Glue only triangle shapes on a piece of triangular paper. Do other shapes in the same manner.

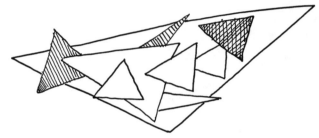

STORE COLLAGE
Select one type of store (pet store, candy store, grocery store, toy store, etc.). Draw or cut out magazine pictures of things found in that store. Glue the pictures onto a piece of paper or cardboard. Make a store sign on top.

TAKE A TRIP COLLAGE
Cut a large piece of paper or cardboard into the shape of a suitcase. Draw or cut out magazine pictures of things taken on a trip. Glue pictures onto the cardboard suitcase. Don't forget the toothbrush!

A RED COLLAGE
Glue only red things on a piece of red paper. It's surprising how many different shades of red there are. Color the glue red, too! Do other colors in the same manner. After all other colors have been done, make a rainbow collage.

COLORED RICE

SUPPLIES
- rice (uncooked)
- powdered tempera paint
- containers for mixing rice
- glue in glue cup
- glue brush
- spoon
- paper

PREPARATION
- Pour rice in container and add a little powdered tempera paint. Stir until the rice and paint are mixed. Repeat for each color desired.
- Pour glue into glue cup.

LET'S BEGIN
1. Brush a design on paper with glue.
2. Take a spoon and sprinkle colored rice over glued area.
3. Pour excess rice off of paper and back into container.
4. Brush on more glue and add another color.
5. When picture is finished, dry flat.

OTHER IDEAS
- Try coloring cornmeal, oatmeal, salt or other grains and glue in the same manner.
- Rice can also be colored with food color, water and a few drops of alcohol. Let sit for a few minutes, then drain off colored water. Spread colored rice on wax paper to dry.

State of Tennessee
By Jamie

EGGSHELL MOSAICS

SUPPLIES
- broken eggshells
- watercolor paint
- brushes
- glue
- paper

PREPARATION
- Wash eggshells thoroughly and break into small pieces.

LET'S BEGIN
1. Glue broken pieces of eggshells on a piece of paper.
2. Let eggshells dry for a few minutes.
3. Paint the eggshells with watercolor paints to finish the picture.
4. Put picture away to dry and wash brushes.

OTHER IDEAS
- Gluing eggshells on dark paper tends to emphasize the color of paints chosen.
- Try coloring the eggshells before gluing them. Mix a few drops of food color and water in a container. Add the eggshells and let sit for a few minutes. Strain the water and spread the eggshells out flat to dry.

CAUTION
- Make sure the eggshells have been cleaned thoroughly to avoid possible **Salmonella** poisoning.

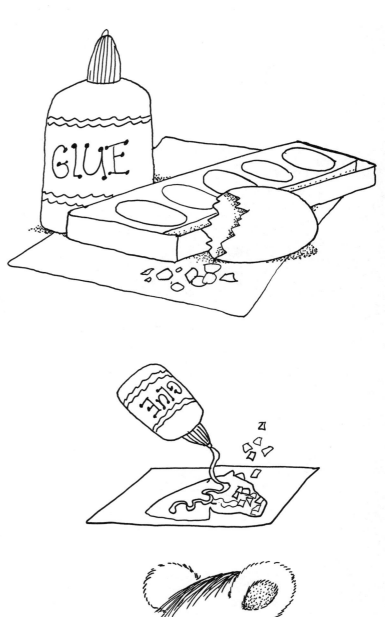

ANIMAL CRACKERS

SUPPLIES
- animal crackers
- glue
- glue cup
- glue brush
- markers
- paper

PREPARATION
- Pour glue into glue cup.

LET'S BEGIN
1. Pick out a few animal crackers.
2. Glue crackers on a piece of paper.
3. Using the markers, color stripes, dots and faces on the crackers.
4. Draw details such as cages, animal food and scenery on the background paper.
5. Allow picture to dry and wash glue brushes.

OTHER IDEAS
- Make an animal circus train. Cut pieces of paper into rectangles for train cars. Glue on animal crackers and draw vertical striped lines to depict cages. Glue or draw on circles for wheels.

CAUTION
- Make sure children do not eat the used animal crackers.

PAPER PLATE MASKS

SUPPLIES
- paper plates
- glue in glue cup
- glue brush
- scissors
- scrap papers and collage pieces
- markers or paint
- string, elastic or a tongue depressor

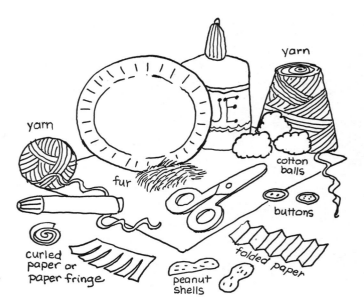

PREPARATION
- Cut two eyeholes in paper plate.
- Assemble all collage pieces.
- Pour glue in glue cup.

LET'S BEGIN
1. Using various scrap materials, cut out eyes, nose, mouth, teeth, ears, hair, beard, horns, earrings, etc. and glue them on a paper plate.
2. Using markers or paints, color in the exposed areas of the paper plate.
3. Secure a piece of string or elastic on the sides to wear as a mask. Or, stick a tongue depressor on the bottom of the plate for a handle.

OTHER IDEAS
- Instead of a paper plate, use a large grocery bag to create a mask that can be worn over the head.

47

MAGIC PAPER

SUPPLIES
- colored tissue
- glue
- water
- container for glue/water
- brush
- paper

PREPARATION
- Cut tissue into small size pieces.
- Mix glue and water into a solution the consistency of liquid starch.

LET'S BEGIN
1. Brush a piece of paper with the glue/water solution.
2. Choose pieces of colored tissue and stick on the paper.
3. Overlap the various shapes and colors to create new colors and shapes.
4. After the tissue has been adhered to the paper, apply another coat of glue/water.
5. Wash out brush and let paper dry.

OTHER IDEAS
- Tissue paper will bleed when it is wet thus creating a painting without paints. Follow the directions for magic paper but peel off the tissue after applying the second coat of glue/water. The color from the tissue will be left on the paper.
- Boxes, jars and plastic lids can be decorated in this same manner. When glue is dry, spray the entire article with a clear enamel to preserve.

STAMP, INK AND ROLL

STAMPERS

There are many types of stampers to choose from for printmaking but the process is generally the same for all of them.

PROCESS FOR MAKING PRINTS

- Make a print by stamping the stamper on an ink pad and then pressing it on some paper. If an ink pad is not available, soak a sponge in liquid tempera and place in a flat dish.

- Another method that can be used is to brush the ink or paint on a stamper and print as above. By doing it this way, more than one color can be brushed on at a time for interesting details.
- Paint with the same object many times until the desired pattern is finished. Continuing to print without re-inking will cause the imprints to be progressively lighter.

- Encourage the use of a variety of colors and stampers. Try overlapping the different shapes.
- Print designs, borders, and patterns with stampers or combine several styles to make planned pictures.
- Stamping is great for making personalized wrapping paper and greeting cards.

BODY STAMPERS

SUPPLIES
- fingers, toes, hands, feet
- stamp pads or tempera in flat dish
- paper

LET'S BEGIN
1. Stamp finger, side of hand, knuckles, etc., in ink or paint and print onto paper. Try opening and closing fingers for interesting effects.
2. When the picture is finished, use a felt-tip pen or marker and add details to the body prints.

OTHER IDEAS
- Cut out printed pictures and create a collage. What does its shape suggest?

spools

erasers

washers

old puzzle pieces

jar lids

gears

toothpicks

old game pieces

coins

buttons and beads

cork

wood scraps - irregular & geometric shapes

natural items: flowers, leaves, sticks, knotholes, nutshells, etc.

paper clips

GADGET STAMPERS

SUPPLIES
- all kinds of gadgets for stamping
- ink pads or tempera in a flat dish
- paper

LET'S BEGIN
1. Press gadget to be printed into the ink and print onto the paper.
2. Print with the same shape several times before switching to a different gadget stamper.
3. Choose many colors to make an interesting picture.
4. Combine stampers into a design or a planned picture.

CAUTION
- Make sure all gadgets chosen are safe for students to use.

51

FRUIT AND VEGGIE STAMPERS

SUPPLIES
- raw fruits and vegetables (use the parts that would normally be discarded such as the ends of carrots, tops of green peppers, end of celery bunch)
- ink pad or tempera paint in a flat dish
- paper
- knife (for adult use only)

string bean

celery makes the letter "C"

lemon, lime or orange

PREPARATION
- Pre-cut selected fruits and vegetables so the insides will be apparent.

LET'S BEGIN
1. Dip vegetable or fruit into ink or paint.
2. Print onto paper until picture is finished. Take note of the details created by seeds, stems and insides.

OTHER IDEAS
- Use hard vegetables such as potatoes, carrots, or turnips and pre-cut them into a variety of simple geometric shapes. Try printing them together to create new designs.
- Slice a potato in half. Cut a design or picture into the surface with a pencil or pointed object. Print as usual.
- If the fruits and vegetables are left out to dry overnight they will be less juicy and will print better.

cut apple in half to find seeds and "star"

onion

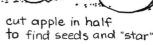

WOOD BLOCK STAMPERS

These stampers can be made by the students and used for printing on another day, or the teacher can make them prior to a stamping session.

RUBBER SHAPE STAMPERS

Cut a piece of an old inner tube (usually found at a garage or junkyard) or spongy insulation tape into simple shapes. Glue the rubber shapes onto a piece of wood or cardboard. Let dry thoroughly before using.

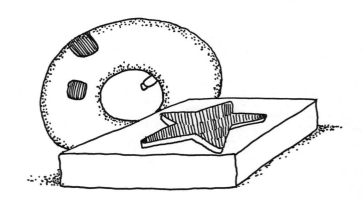

RUBBER BAND STAMPERS

Cut rubber bands of varying widths into different lengths. Glue onto the wood or cardboard piece in an interesting design, letters, shapes, words or numbers. Let dry thoroughly before using.

STRING STAMPERS

Cut a piece of yarn or string. Cover the top of the wood or cardboard with glue. Lay the string on the glue to form a design. Press down gently. Let dry thoroughly before using. When making letters, be sure to glue them on backwards.

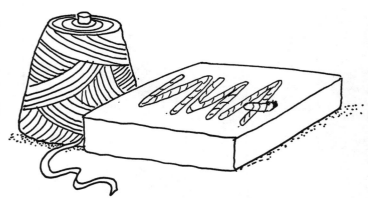

CAUTION
- When washing stamper don't leave it to soak or it will come apart.

SPONGE STAMPERS

SUPPLIES
- sponges
- scissors
- tempera paint in a flat dish
- paper
- water

LET'S BEGIN
1. Cut the sponge into different shapes and sizes. (Pre-cut the shapes for very young children.)
2. Dip the sponge shapes into paint and print onto paper.
3. Try printing with both wet and dry sponge shapes.
4. When finished, wash sponge shapes and let dry.

OTHER IDEAS
- Try using different types of sponges, sponge rubber or Styrofoam.

CLAY STAMPERS

SUPPLIES
- any type of self-hardening clay
- rolling pin
- cookie cutters (optional)
- pointed utensil such as a pencil

LET'S BEGIN
1. Take small pieces of clay and form them into shapes.
2. Use the rolling pin to flatten these to a thickness of about ½".
3. Use a pointed utensil to scratch designs into the soft clay.
4. Let clay harden and use as printers.

OTHER IDEAS
- Use cookie cutters to cut out the clay shapes before scratching in designs. Let clay dry and use as printers.
- To produce just the outlines of these stampers use the cookie cutters themselves as stampers.
- Make a number of little clay balls. After they harden, glue them onto the backs of the stampers to use as handles.

ROLLER PRINTERS

Roller printers can be made by students and used after they are thoroughly dry. This may take overnight.

SUPPLIES
- cylinders for printers (cardboard dowels, rolling pins, spools, tin cans, pencils, wooden dowels, etc.)
- string, yarn, inner tube rubber, thin cardboard, etc.
- scissors
- glue
- tempera paint

LET'S BEGIN
1. If using string or yarn, cover the cylinder with glue and wrap the string or yarn around it either in spirals, crisscrosses, or in railroad fashion.
2. If using thin cardboard or inner tube rubber, cut out thin shapes and glue them onto the cylinder.
3. Dip roller printer in a flat dish of tempera paint and roll out the print.

OTHER IDEAS
- Try gluing different textured materials on the cylinder for additional designs.

CAUTION
- If using tin cans make sure there are no sharp edges.

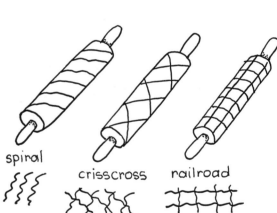

spiral   crisscross   railroad

RELIEF BLOCKS

There are two methods for making relief block printers. One way of doing it is carving or incising a design in the surface of the printing block (or plate), inking and printing. The ink will cover the background leaving the incised lines the color of the paper printed on. The second method of making a relief block is to build up a collage surface (sometimes called a collograph) from an assortment of paper, cardboard, string, material scraps, etc. The ink will be absorbed by the different textural surfaces raised up on the plate leaving the background its original color.

INKING YOUR RELIEF BLOCK

Both types of relief blocks can be printed the same way.

SUPPLIES

- water base printing ink (oil base needs to be cleaned with turpentine or mineral spirits)
- flat tray, cookie sheet or piece of floor tile
- brayer (roller)
- paper

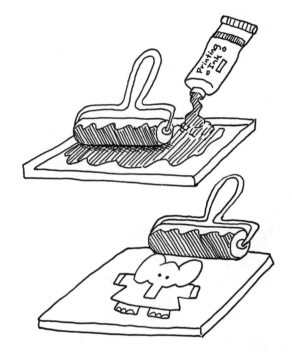

LET'S BEGIN

1. Squeeze a small amount of ink onto the tray.
2. Roll it out with a brayer until it is smooth.
3. Roll the inked brayer over the relief block from side to side and top to bottom. Cover the entire surface evenly.
4. Place a piece of paper onto the inked block and rub gently with fingers.
5. Peel off paper to see print.
6. Re-ink the block for another print.

OTHER IDEAS

- If a brayer or printer's ink are not available for use, brush liquid tempera paint on the block and print as above.

INCISED RELIEF BLOCKS

SOAP

Smooth one side of a large bar of soap with a scraper to make sure the painting surface is flat. Carve a design into the soap with a sharp pencil or dowel sharpened in a pencil sharpener. Ink and print.

STYROFOAM MEAT TRAY

Wash a Styrofoam meat tray from the grocery store and cut off the curved edges. Draw or indent a design into the surface with a pencil or sharpened dowel. Ink and print.

CORRUGATED CARDBOARD

Cut large pieces of corrugated cardboard from a cardboard box. Draw a design into the surface of the cardboard with a pen. You can also remove pieces of the cardboard surface to leave the corrugated bumps as another printing surface. Ink and print.

PLASTER BLOCK

Mix molding plaster by following the directions on the box. Pour it into a shallow dish. Remove when dry. This will be the plaster block. Carve a design into the plaster surface with a sharpened dowel, paper clip or nail. Ink and print.

OTHER IDEAS

- Letters, names and words are fun to incise in these blocks. Remember to make them in reverse.

RAISED RELIEF BLOCKS

STYROFOAM

Cut a Styrofoam meat tray into various shapes and sizes. Glue these pieces onto another Styrofoam tray or a piece of cardboard, making sure surface is relatively flat. Dry thoroughly. Ink and print.

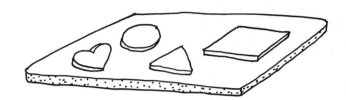

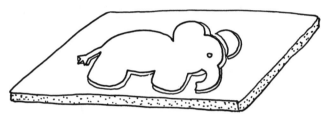

CARDBOARD

Cut a variety of shapes from a piece of cardboard. Glue these onto a cardboard background. Dry thoroughly. Ink and print.

GLUE LINES

Pour white school glue into a squeeze bottle. Squeeze glue onto a piece of cardboard or wood to create different designs and patterns. Let dry thoroughly. Ink and print.

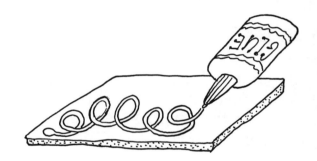

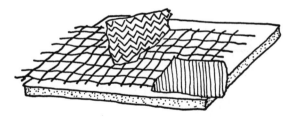

MATERIAL SCRAPS

Choose pieces of materials that have various textures, preferably open weave materials such as burlap. Cut these into different shapes and glue them onto a cardboard background. Dry thoroughly. Ink and print.

STRING

Glue different widths of string and yarn on a cardboard background in a free design. Let dry thoroughly. Ink and print.

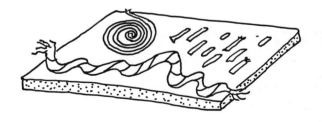

OTHER IDEAS

- Discarded cereal and cracker boxes are good sources of cardboard for these printing blocks.

MONO PRINTING

Unlike the printing blocks previously mentioned, a mono print is generally good for only a single print. The mono print block must be made over again before reprinting.

SUPPLIES
- pane of glass with edges taped (If unavailable, a piece of Formica, cookie sheet, or other smooth, non-absorbent hard surface will do.)
- tempera paint
- paper
- scissors
- cotton swabs (optional)
- water

BASIC MONO PRINT
Spread paint or ink over glass plate. Use your finger or a cotton swab to make lines and designs in the ink. Place a piece of paper over the paint. Press gently. Pull up for a print.

STENCILED MONO PRINT
Spread paint or ink over the glass plate. Cut out paper shapes and lay on top of painted plate. Place a sheet of paper over paper shapes. Press gently. Lift up for a print.

PAINT MONO PRINT
Paint a picture on the glass plate. Let dry. Dampen a sheet of paper. Place paper over painted plate and press gently. Pull up for a print.

HANGING BY A THREAD

STRINGING ODDS AND ENDS

SUPPLIES

- string or yarn
- a large tapestry needle or a bobby pin with the ends taped
- any combination of treasures such as those listed below

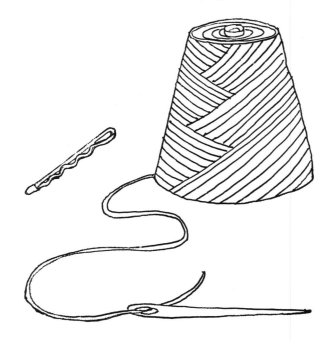

> **Seashells** with holes in them
> **Styrofoam** packing pieces
> **Paper letters and numbers**
> **Acorn tops**
> **Drinking straws** cut into different lengths
> **Spools** (Paint before or after stringing.)
> **Paper shapes** (Use wallpaper, too!) Punch holes for easier threading.
> **Buttons**
> **Beads**
> **Veggies and fruits** such as potato slices, carrot slices, orange peels, etc. String and let dry in the sun for interesting changes in shapes.
> **Uncooked macaroni** of different sizes and shapes (Color these by placing them in a container of food color, water and a few drops of alcohol. Let this sit for a few minutes. Then drain off colored water and spread out macaroni to dry.)

LET'S BEGIN

1. Cut a length of string about 18" and tie a large knot at the end.
2. Choose items to be strung and thread these onto a piece of yarn or string. Tie the ends together when finished.

OTHER IDEAS

- If a needle is not available, cover the end of the yarn with tape or dip it into paraffin wax or glue and let it harden.

EDIBLE STRINGS

These strings are great fun because they can be eaten either during or after the activity!

SUPPLIES
- string or yarn
- large tapestry needle
- any combination of foods such as those listed below

OTHER IDEAS
- For additional eating, string foods on pieces of shoestring licorice.

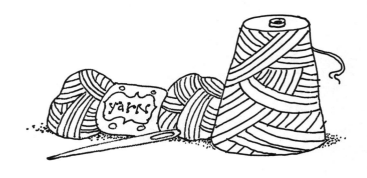

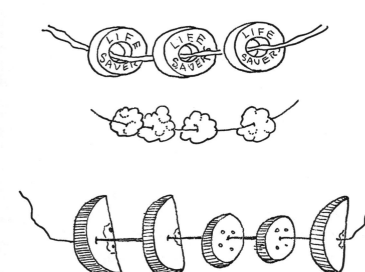

- **"Fruitloops"**, **"Cheerios"**, or any cereal with a "hole"
- **Popcorn**
- **Marshmallows** (regular or multi-colored) The needle gets sticky fast so keep a paper towel handy to wipe it off.
- **Apple slices** (or your favorite fruit or veggie) Dip in lemon juice before stringing to keep them from turning brown.
- **"Life Savers"** (assorted fruit flavors are the favorite)
- **Gumdrops** and Gumdrop Rings
- **Edible Bead Dough** (see recipe below)

EDIBLE BEAD DOUGH
Heat 1½ tsp. unflavored gelatin and ¼ C. water in double boiler until gelatin dissolves. Cool. Gradually stir in 1 box powdered sugar. Knead until smooth. This hardens fast when exposed to air so keep it in plastic until ready to use and string each bead as you make it.

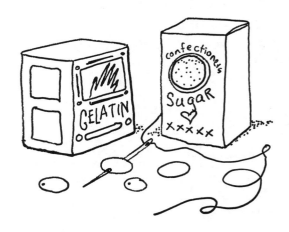

HOMEMADE BEADS

SALT PUTTY BEADS

Mix thoroughly ⅔ cup salt, ½ cup flour, ½ cup water and food color. Mold beads by rolling and shaping. Make a hole with a toothpick. Air dry on foil or wax paper.

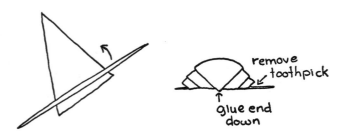

remove toothpick

glue end down

PAPER CLIP BEADS

Make a long chain by hooking paper clips together. Cut a short and narrow piece of colored tape or contact paper and wrap it around the middle of each paper clip. (Paper clips are available in assorted sizes, shapes and colors.)

CORNSTARCH CLAY BEADS

Mix 1 cup salt and ½ cup cornstarch in top of double boiler. Slowly add ¾ cup water. Heat until thick and cool on a piece of foil. Make beads by rolling or shaping. Make a hole with a toothpick. Air dry on foil or wax paper.

PAPER ROLL-UP BEADS

Cut long thin triangles from colored paper or magazine pages. Lay a toothpick at base of triangle. Roll up paper with toothpick still inside. Glue end of triangle down. When dry remove toothpick. String several papers together to make a chain.

BREAD AND GLUE BEADS

Tear slices of bread into small pieces. Add glue and a couple drops of lemon juice (about 3 tbs. glue to 4 slices of bread). Stir together. Knead until soft. Make beads by shaping. Make holes with a toothpick. Let them harden by air drying (this usually takes 1-2 days). Paint when hardened. This is a good way to use up bread crusts and unused bread.

SEWING

SUPPLIES
- large tapestry needle
- yarns of different colors
- materials such as those below

OPEN WEAVE MATERIAL

Cut a piece of burlap to desired size. Thread the needle and practice sewing through the holes in the burlap using a straight running stitch. For planned designs, draw lines on the burlap with a marker and sew along the lines. When finished, tape the top of the burlap over a dowel and hang with a piece of yarn.

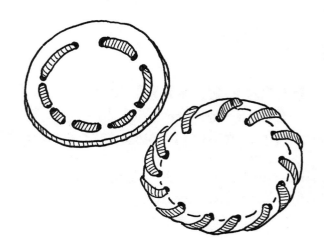

STYROFOAM TRAY

Punch holes to make a design in the meat tray. Thread needle and sew using a straight running stitch until entire design is completed. (This is similar to connect-the-dots drawing activities. If students have an understanding of numbers, write numbers in consecutive order next to the punched holes.) Color with markers or paints when finished.

PLASTIC LID

Punch holes around the edge of the plastic lid (or plate). Thread needle and sew in and out of holes in a straight running stitch, or around the edge of lid, sewing under, up and around. Color lid with paints or markers when finished sewing, if desired.

WEAVING

PAPER WEAVING

Cut strips of paper in a variety of widths. Fold a piece of paper in half and cut slits making sure to leave about 1" borders. Open the folded paper and weave the paper strips through the slits. Hold strips in place with a dot of glue. To make interesting weavings, cut slits and strips in zigzag or wavy lines.

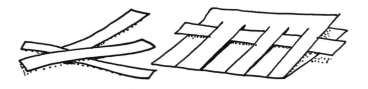

PAPER PLATE WEAVING

Make a hole in the middle of a paper plate. Cut an uneven number of slits around perimeter of plate. Thread the loom by wrapping a string up through the middle hole and around a slit. Pull up through the middle and around the next slit. Continue until all slits have been wrapped. To weave, start at center of loom and weave a piece of yarn over and under the string until the weaving is finished. Tie the string end to loom.

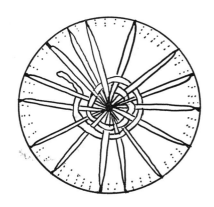

NATURAL WEAVING

Choose a small tree branch or piece of driftwood in the shape of a 'Y'. Cut several pieces of string and tie both ends onto the arms to make a loom. Weave yarns, or natural materials such as grasses, vines, and flowers, over and under the threaded loom.

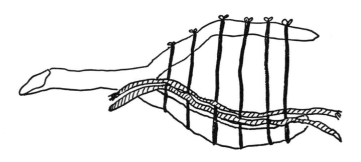

BERRY BASKET WEAVING

Cut a piece of brightly colored yarn and cover the end with tape or paraffin. Weave in and out of the spaces in a plastic berry basket, continuing around all sides until weaving is completed.

CONSTRUCTION WORK

REUSABLE MODELING CLAY

COOKED MODELING CLAY
3 C. flour
1½ C. salt
6 tbs. oil
3 C. water
6 tsp. cream of tartar
food color

Mix above ingredients and stir over medium heat until clay leaves the side of pan. Stir continuously, making sure there are no lumps. Let cool. Store in a covered container when not in use.

NON-COOKED MODELING CLAY
2 C. flour
1 C. salt
½ C. water
food color

Mix above ingredients. Knead to work in color and remove bumps. Store in an airtight container when not in use.

Students can mold the clay into figures or bowls using hands and fingers. They can also enjoy experimenting with different tools.

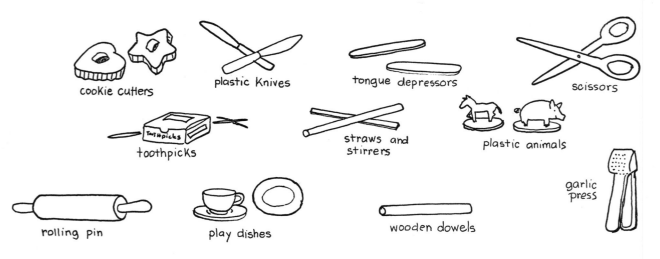

cookie cutters

plastic knives

tongue depressors

scissors

toothpicks

straws and stirrers

plastic animals

rolling pin

play dishes

wooden dowels

garlic press

SELF-HARDENING CLAY

SALT AND FLOUR CLAY

1 C. salt
1 C. flour
1 tbs. powdered alum
water
mixing bowl
food color (optional)

Mix salt, flour and alum with enough water to make the consistency of putty. Mold into figures, animals or pots. Let air dry until hard. Paint with tempera paints or watercolors, if desired.

Applying a final coat of shellac to the hardened clay pieces will help to preserve the finish. Make sure the room is well ventilated when shellacking.

SAWDUST CLAY

2 parts sawdust
1 part wheat paste*
water

Mix wheat paste and sawdust with enough water to make a pliable mixture. Mold into desired figures and let air dry.

*To make your own wheat paste, mix 1 C. flour and 3 C. water. Stir over medium heat until it starts to boil. Take off heat and let cool.

BAKED MODELING CLAY

BAKER'S CLAY

4 C. flour
1 C. salt
1½ C. water

Mix flour, salt and water. Knead until smooth, adding extra water if too stiff. Shape clay into figures, animals or letters. Place these figurines on a piece of foil and on a cookie sheet. Bake at 300° for 1 hour. When cool, paint and add shellac for permanence.

BREAD DOUGH

1 package yeast
2 C. warm water
3 tbs. sugar
2 tsp. salt
¼ C. oil
7 C. flour

Mix yeast with sugar and warm water. Let stand for 5 minutes. Add salt and oil. Add flour a little at a time. Knead, adding more flour if sticky. Make a sculpture and transfer it to a piece of foil on a cookie sheet. Keep project simple because the dough will puff and small details won't show. Adhere parts together with a little water. Let rise about 15 minutes. Bake at 350° for about 25 minutes. When cool, add details with paint. Shellac for a shiny surface.

OTHER IDEAS
- To make hanging ornaments, insert a paper clip or a piece of bent wire into the dough before baking.
- Use stampers to stamp in the clay before baking. Make sure to dip stamper in flour to prevent sticking.

EDIBLE MODELING CLAY

PEANUT BUTTER CLAY

peanut butter
dry milk
wax paper
bowl
spoon

Mix peanut butter with dry milk so that it can be molded without being sticky. Put on wax paper and play with it like clay. To keep fingers from getting too sticky, periodically dip them into a bowl of dry milk. When finished, eat the clay! Discard leftovers.

PRETZELS

1 package yeast
1½ C. warm water
1 tbs. sugar
1 tsp. salt
4 C. flour
1 egg (beaten)
kosher salt

Mix yeast, water, salt and sugar. Stir in flour. Knead dough on table. Shape into animals, figures or letters. Brush with egg and sprinkle on kosher salt. Place on cookie sheet. Bake at 425° for 12-15 minutes. These taste best when they are still warm.

PAPIER-MÂCHÉ

SUPPLIES
- wheat paste (see recipe under Sawdust Clay)
- newspapers
- scissors
- containers for wheat paste (aluminum pie tin)
- tempera paint
- brushes
- tape (optional but handy)

PREPARATION
- Make wheat paste and pour into container.
- Cut or tear strips of newspaper (about 1" x 5").
- Cut pages of newspaper in half to use as base.

LET'S BEGIN
1. Crumple or roll newspaper and form it into figures such as animals, people or abstract forms.
2. Use tape to attach adjoining pieces.
3. Dip one paper strip at a time into the wheat paste and wrap around the newspaper form.
4. Continue wrapping dipped newspaper strips until the figure is covered. It is best to make it at least two layers thick. Smooth all wrinkles and bumps.
5. Allow papier-mâché form to dry about 2-3 days.
6. Paint the form as desired with tempera paint. A final coat of shellac will help preserve it and make it shine.

72

PAPIER-MÂCHÉ FORMS

Papier-mâché can cover almost anything. Instead of covering a form made from newspaper try covering:

CARDBOARD DOWEL

Cut cardboard paper towel and toilet tissue dowels into various lengths. Tape together into a base form. Cover the entire form with papier-mâché strips. Allow to dry thoroughly. Paint and decorate.

BALLOON

Inflate a balloon to desired size and tie it closed. Apply papier-mâché strips onto the balloon until entire surface is covered. Allow to dry thoroughly. Pop the balloon with a pin. Paint and decorate. This can also be cut in half and used for masks.

PLASTIC BOTTLE

Choose a plastic bottle for a form and tape on rolled up newspapers for additional features. Apply papier-mâché strips to cover entire form. Let dry. Paint and decorate with buttons, yarns, material scraps, etc.

PLASTIC BOWL

Turn a plastic bowl upside down and cover the outside surface with a film of Vaseline or Crisco. Apply papier-mâché strips directly on greased outer surface until entire surface is covered. The more layers you apply the sturdier it will be. Allow to dry, then remove the plastic bowl. Paint and decorate.

CARDBOARD BOXES

Choose small boxes and attach together with tape. Cover the entire surface with papier-mâché strips. Smooth the corners. Let dry. Paint and decorate with beads, buttons, etc.

OTHER WAYS WITH PAPIER-MÂCHÉ

PAPIER-MÂCHÉ SANDWICH

This works well with very young children who have difficulty wrapping strips around a form.

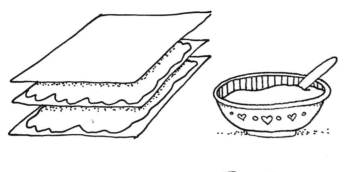

- Cut pages of newspapers into pieces about 12" x 14".
- Make a "sandwich" by spreading wheat paste between about six sheets of the newspaper. (See recipe for wheat paste under Sawdust Clay.)
- Cut a simple shape out of this sandwich. Make sure to wash off scissors before wheat paste dries!
- Punch a hole near the top to hang. Let dry 2-3 days. Paint, decorate and hang shape when dry.

PAPIER-MÂCHÉ PULP

This papier-mâché can be used effectively with young children because the method is not used for covering forms, but for modeling.

Monday afternoon

Wednesday morning

- Tear newspapers into small pieces about ½"-1" square.
- Place these torn papers into a container and cover with water, making sure all paper gets wet.
- For each quart of paper/water mixture add a teaspoon of salt to prevent spoiling. Let soak for 36 hours.
- Mix and squeeze mixture until it turns mushy. Add a small amount of wheat paste and continue to mix and squeeze.
- Make a form by modeling this mixture. Allow to dry thoroughly.
- When dry, paint and decorate.

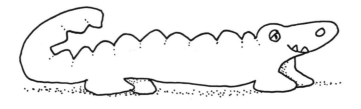

SPAGHETTI SCULPTURES

SUPPLIES
- raw spaghetti
- glue in a squeeze bottle
- wax paper

LET'S BEGIN
1. Break spaghetti into various lengths.
2. Lay a few strands of spaghetti in a crisscross fashion on a piece of wax paper.
3. Apply glue to the points where the spaghetti crosses.
4. Let dry.
5. Repeat this process two more times to make a total of three flat spaghetti units.
6. When these units are dry, arrange and glue them into a three-dimensional structure.

FOIL FORMS

SUPPLIES
- aluminum foil
- transparent tape
- tempera paint
- liquid detergent
- brush
- container for paint

PREPARATION
- Mix a few drops of liquid detergent with tempera paint.
- Tear foil into various sizes.

LET'S BEGIN
1. Mold foil into individual forms by crumpling, twisting, and pinching.
2. Join these pieces together either by pinching the foil or by taping.
3. Continue adding foil pieces until the sculpture is complete.
4. When finished, paint the sculpture using tempera paint mixed with liquid detergent. Let dry.

WIRE TWISTS

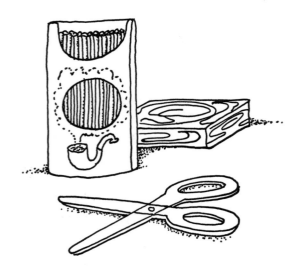

SUPPLIES
- assorted colors of pipe cleaners
- scissors
- base such as wood block or Styrofoam block (optional)

LET'S BEGIN
1. Bend and twist a pipe cleaner into a desired shape.
2. A sculpture can be done with just one length of pipe cleaner or it can consist of several lengths joined together. Hook additional pieces on by winding and twisting.
3. To create coiled shapes, wind the wire around objects such as pencils, pill bottles or sticks.
4. Stick finished sculpture into a base so that it can stand upright.

OTHER IDEAS
- To add detail, glue material, paper or felt scraps onto the finished pipe cleaner sculpture.
- Colored telephone wire works just as well as pipe cleaners. Try obtaining some from a telephone repair person.

SAND CASTING

SUPPLIES
- sand
- plaster of Paris
- box to hold sand sculpture
- water
- spoon
- bucket or bowl for mixing plaster

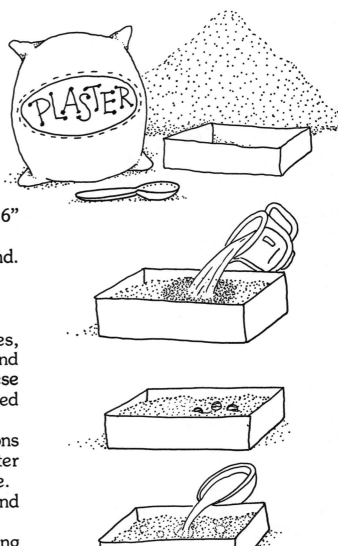

PREPARATION
- Fill a cardboard box with sand at least 6" deep.
- Add a little water to dampen the sand. (It should be firm but not runny.)

LET'S BEGIN
1. Press objects (spoons, fingers, marbles, shells, cookie cutters, etc.) into the sand to form depressions. Remember, these depressions will form the shape of finished sculpture.
2. Mix plaster of Paris according to directions on package, adding plaster to the water and stirring until mixture is lump-free.
3. Carefully pour the plaster into the sand indentions made earlier.
4. To hang the shape, insert a loop of string or wire into the top.
5. Let air dry overnight. Remove from box, making sure to brush off any loose sand.

OTHER IDEAS
- Add a few drops of food color to the plaster before pouring into the sand mold to make a colored sand sculpture.

CAUTION
- Never pour plaster down the drain as it hardens rather quickly. Throw all leftover plaster in the garbage.

EDIBLE CONSTRUCTIONS

VEGGIE CREATIONS

SUPPLIES

- assorted vegetables
- toothpicks
- knife

Cut vegetables into small pieces. Attach these pieces to a larger vegetable with toothpicks. When finished, eat!

APPLE HEADS

SUPPLIES

- apples
- peanut butter or cream cheese
- a variety of toppings

Cut apple into cross sections about ½" wide. Spread on peanut butter or cream cheese. Add toppings to make silly faces and then eat!

GRAHAM CRACKER CONSTRUCTION

SUPPLIES

- wax paper
- graham crackers
- frosting glue

Make frosting glue by mixing 3 egg whites, 1 box confectioners' sugar, ½ tsp. salt and 1 tbs. lemon juice. Beat until it holds its shape and forms peaks.

Cut or break graham crackers into smaller rectangles, squares and triangles. Use frosting glue to attach them together into a flat design or a stand-up construction. Add cake and cookie decorations to the finished product and then eat!

TOOTHPICK TOWERS

Gluing toothpicks together into a sculpture can be quite frustrating for young children, but they can use them to hold small items together to make buildings, animals, and abstract structures.

SUPPLIES

- toothpicks (the round type work best and also come in colors)
- small objects such as: (marshmallows, raisins, chick peas, Styrofoam packing pieces, small balls of clay)

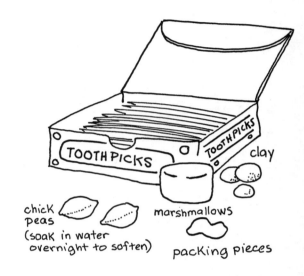

chick peas (soak in water overnight to soften)

marshmallows

packing pieces

clay

LET'S BEGIN

1. Insert toothpick into a small object.
2. Connect to other small objects until sculpture is finished.
3. To build a high structure, make sure to build a sturdy base such as a triangle or square shape.
4. For a special finish, spray paint the entire structure. (This should be done by an adult in a well ventilated area.)

OTHER IDEAS

- Use pieces of spaghetti instead of toothpicks.

STARCHED STRING

SUPPLIES
- string or yarn
- flour
- water
- container for paste (aluminum pie tin)
- wax paper
- tissue paper (optional)
- scissors
- spoon

PREPARATION
- Make flour and water paste by mixing together until it is the consistency of heavy cream.
- Cut string in various lengths.

LET'S BEGIN
1. Dip a length of the string into the flour and water paste so it is completely covered.
2. Arrange the string into an interesting shape on the wax paper.
3. Continue dipping and adding string until sculpture is completed.
4. Let the string dry overnight.
5. When the string is dry, cover some of the open areas with tissue paper to create a stained glass effect.
6. Hang finished project with a piece of string.

OTHER IDEAS
- This project may be done more three-dimensionally by wrapping the dipped string around an inflated balloon. When the string is dry, pop the balloon.

CONTAINER CREATIONS

SUPPLIES

- empty containers of all shapes and sizes (Make sure they are safe and clean.)
- glue and/or tape
- scissors
- tempera paint
- liquid detergent
- brush
- container for paint
- scrap materials (optional)

LET'S BEGIN

1. Have the artist choose suitable containers.
2. Glue or tape the containers together to form animals, people, automobiles, buildings or abstract designs. Cut away pieces if needed.
3. Add a few drops of liquid detergent to the tempera paint. Add colors and details to creations.
4. Other scrap materials can also be glued on for hair, eyes, clothes, etc.

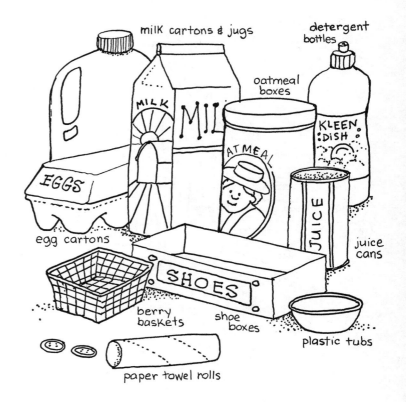

WOOD SCRAPS

SUPPLIES
- wood scraps
- glue
- paints, markers or crayons
- brush

LET'S BEGIN
1. Choose a few pieces of wood scraps and arrange/build them into animals, robots, buildings or abstract structures. The construction can be very small or super large. (For example, make a large spaceship with small space creatures to fit inside.)
2. When the arrangement of wood scraps is complete, glue together and let dry.
3. Use crayons, markers or paint to add finishing details.

OTHER IDEAS
- Check with local lumberyards for free or inexpensive wood scraps.
- Wooden plugs (for covering screws) make wonderful headlights and push buttons. They can be purchased at a hardware or woodworker's store.
- It's fun to make a village or city using wood scraps. Take a large piece of heavy cardboard and draw roads with a marker. Make individual buildings, tunnels, bridges, etc., and glue them to the board. Use a small car or make your own and drive through the tiny city.

MESS-ABOUTS

DROPPERS

SUPPLIES

- medicine droppers (cleaned thoroughly)
- food colors
- water
- containers for colors (three)
- ice cube tray (preferably clear or white)

PREPARATION

- Pour water into three small containers. Add a few drops of food color to each one. Make one red, one blue and one yellow.
- Half fill ice cube tray with water.

LET'S BEGIN

1. Fill the medicine dropper with one color and squeeze the drops into one of the compartments in the ice cube tray.
2. Squeeze other colors in the tray to mix and make new colors. Try to make orange, purple and green.
3. When all the compartments in the ice cube tray are full, empty and start over, or put tray in the freezer to make colored ice cubes. When frozen, take the tray out of the freezer and watch the cubes melt into colored puddles.

OTHER IDEAS

- Use fruit juices instead of colored water and mix them in the same manner. Freeze and use fruit cubes for a snack.
- Instead of ice cube trays, drop the colored water directly on white paper towels or napkins.
- Produce the opposite effect to the above by dropping bleach mixed with water onto colored tissue paper. Be careful with this activity as bleach is toxic.

DIP AND TWIST

SUPPLIES
- water
- food colors
- containers for colored water
- white paper towels or napkins

PREPARATION
- Pour water into small containers and add a few drops of food color. You should make containers of the primary colors - red, yellow, blue.

LET'S BEGIN
1. Fold a white paper towel into halves, then quarters.
2. Dip a corner of the folded towel into one color of water.
3. Dip another corner of the folded towel into a second color.
4. Repeat until the folded napkin is colored completely.
5. Carefully unfold napkin to see the result.
6. Let dry.

OTHER IDEAS
- Try this activity by twisting the the paper towel instead of folding.
- Wrap a paper towel around a pencil or crayon and secure it with a rubber band. Dip wrapped pencil into the colored water. Take off the rubber band and unwrap to see the design.

SPARKLE PAINTS

SUPPLIES
- squeeze bottles
- flour
- salt
- water
- tempera paint
- paper

PREPARATION
- Mix equal parts of flour, salt and water.
- Divide mixture and pour into squeeze bottles.
- Add a different color tempera paint to each squeeze bottle and shake.

LET'S BEGIN
1. On a sheet of paper, squeeze sparkle paints into a design, picture, words or name.
2. Let paints dry thoroughly. When dry the salt will make the picture sparkle.

OTHER IDEAS
- Sparkle paints can also be brushed on like regular tempera paint.

FLOUR BATIK

Batik is an ancient art of cloth decoration usually done with hot waxes and fabric dyes. This method of batiking is much too dangerous for young children because the hot wax is flammable and the dyes are toxic. Here is a simple batiking process that is safe and fun to do with children.

SUPPLIES
- flour
- water
- squeeze bottle
- piece of white cloth (an old sheet works fine)
- food colors
- containers for colored water
- brushes

PREPARATION
- Mix flour and water together until smooth and creamy and pour into a squeeze bottle.
- In separate containers, mix colored waters as desired.

LET'S BEGIN
1. Squeeze the flour/water mixture into a design on a piece of cloth. (Make lines thick.)
2. Let the flour design dry overnight.
3. When dry, paint over the entire cloth and flour design with the colored waters.
4. When finished painting, scrape the flour designs off the cloth and see the design that was created.

Thursday

Friday

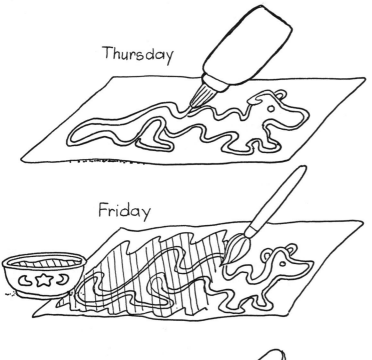

SHAVING CREAM

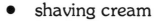

SUPPLIES
- shaving cream
- food colors
- flat trays

LET'S BEGIN
1. Spray shaving cream onto a tray or directly on the surface of the table (if it is Formica covered).
2. Add drops of food color.
3. Mess-about by spreading shaving cream around to create designs and pictures.
4. Write letters and names. Pile the shaving cream up into a mountain.
5. Add drops of other food colors to see what colors they create.
6. Exercise caution when cleaning up as shaving cream tends to be slippery underfoot.

OTHER IDEAS
- This activity is fun to do out-of-doors on a warm day when you can wear your bathing suit. Rub the shaving cream all over your arms, legs and tummies, too!
- Squirt some shaving cream into a Ziploc storage bag and play with this as in Bag Painting. Add a few drops of food color if desired. When finished, put bag in freezer. When shaving cream is frozen, take it out of the bag and feel it melt.

CAUTION
- Shaving cream stings if it gets into the eyes.

SOAP FLAKES

SUPPLIES
- soap flakes
- water
- food colors
- container for mixing
- spoon
- tray or paper

PREPARATION
- Mix two parts soap flakes with one part water until thick and creamy. Add food color if desired. This will be "soap paint."

LET'S BEGIN
1. Put a spoonful of soap paint on either tray or paper and play with it as regular finger paint.
2. If paper is used, allow it to dry when finished.
3. If a tray is used, wash it off carefully as soap is very slippery.

OTHER IDEAS
- Make the soap flake mixture a little thicker and use it like clay to model animals and figures.
- Make soap crayons to write in the sink, water basin or bathtub. To do so, mix soap flakes, water, and food color and pour the mixture into a small container or ice cube tray. Set this in the sun to dry.

CORNSTARCH AND WATER

SUPPLIES
- cornstarch
- water
- food colors
- tray or tin for mixing (such as an aluminum pie tin)

LET'S BEGIN
1. Put a handful of cornstarch onto the tray. Let students feel it while it is still dry.
2. Mix water into the cornstarch until it is thick and smooth.
3. Add a few drops of food color and mix.
4. Make designs in the cornstarch mixture with hands, enjoying the gooey and runny feeling.
5. When the mixture feels like it is starting to dry, pick up some with fingers and watch it melt. (The warmth of your hands turns it back to liquid.)
6. When finished throw used cornstarch in the garbage, not down the drain!

OATMEAL MIXING

SUPPLIES
- oatmeal
- wash basin
- assorted containers, scoops, spoons

PREPARATION
- Pour oatmeal into wash basin.

LET'S BEGIN
1. Mix, stir and pour the oatmeal using containers, scoops and spoons.
2. When finished, pour the oatmeal back into its container and save for another day.

OTHER IDEAS
- Use cornmeal, rice or other grains instead of oatmeal.
- Color the oatmeal by mixing in a little powdered tempera paint.
- Add a little water to the oatmeal for another textural experience.

INDOOR SAND CASTLES

SUPPLIES
- sand
- water
- containers of different sizes and shapes for mixing
- wash basin
- found objects

PREPARATION
- Fill a wash basin with sand.

LET'S BEGIN
1. Pour a little water into the basin until the sand begins to stick together. Don't get it too wet!
2. Mix, pour, and dig, using different containers as well as hands.
3. Make the moistened sand into shapes with your hands or fill containers and tip upside down to make a mold.
4. For finishing touches, add sticks, pebbles, shells, plastic animals, little cars, etc.

OTHER IDEAS
- Keep a small hand broom and dustpan handy so students can clean up any spills.
- Give color to a castle by adding a little powdered tempera paint to the sand.
- More water can be added to create pools or rivers.

INVISIBLE PAINT

SUPPLIES
- water
- paintbrushes
- cans or pails

LET'S BEGIN
1. Fill a can or pail ½ full with water.
2. Paint with the "invisible paint" on the sidewalk, fences, walls or bicycles.
3. What happens as the water paintings dry?

OTHER IDEAS
- Try putting "invisible paint" in squeeze bottles and squeeze designs onto the sidewalk or walls.

MAGIC SHRINKERS

SUPPLIES
- clear plastic lids
- markers
- scissors (optional)
- cookie sheets

LET'S BEGIN
1. Decorate plastic lids with markers.
2. Punch a hole in the top to hang the magic shrinker.
3. Place on a cookie sheet and bake in a 400° oven for about 2-3 minutes.

OTHER IDEAS
- Cut lids into different shapes with scissors before decorating.
- Use Styrofoam meat trays and egg cartons in the same manner.

CAUTION
- Make sure room is well ventilated as the heating of plastic and Styrofoam gives off a gas that could bother people with respiratory disorders.

SNOW PAINTING

SUPPLIES
- snow
- watercolor paints or food colors mixed with water
- brushes
- ladle or spoon
- basin or pail
- tray or flat container such as a pie tin

PREPARATION
- Fill a basin with snow and bring inside.

LET'S BEGIN
1. Spoon some snow from the basin onto a tray. Use a ladle to make a snowball shape.
2. Mold the snow into a miniature sculpture or ball. Wear mittens for this part.
3. When sculpture is finished, paint with watercolors.
4. The indoor snow sculpture only lasts for a short time. It's fun to put it in the sink and watch what happens to the colors as the snow melts.

OTHER IDEAS
- Snow painting can also be done outside where it will last longer. Follow the same procedure as above, only leave finished snow sculpture outside and watch it melt on a sunny day.
- Try filling squeeze bottles with water and food colors and squeeze colored designs onto the snow.
- Scrape frost from a freezer to paint snow during the summertime.

BUBBLES

SUPPLIES
- water
- liquid detergent
- glycerine (purchased at a drug-store)
- sugar
- pipe cleaners
- cookie sheets or tray

PREPARATION
- Make bubble mix by adding 2 tbs. liquid detergent, 1 tbs. glycerine and ½ tsp. sugar into 1 cup water.
- Pour the bubble mix into the cookie sheet.

LET'S BEGIN
1. Have students make their own bubble maker by twisting a pipe cleaner into a "bubble pipe."
2. Dip into bubble mix and blow.
3. Use other bubble makers such as those below.

string & straw frame

berry baskets for multiple bubbles

juice cans with bottoms cut out

paper cups with holes or bottoms cut off

fork

string with ends tied together

straws for blowing in bubble mixture